Extreme
Waterskiing Moves

By Mary Firestone

Consultant:
Scott N. Atkinson
Director of Communications
Editor, *The Water Skier*
USA Water Ski

CAPSTONE
HIGH-INTEREST
BOOKS

an imprint of Capstone Press
Mankato, Minnesota

Capstone High-Interest Books are published by Capstone Press
151 Good Counsel Drive, P.O. Box 669, Mankato, Minnesota 56002
http://www.capstone-press.com

Library of Congress Cataloging-in-Publication Data
Firestone, Mary.
    Extreme waterskiing moves / by Mary Firestone
    p.cm.—(Behind the moves)
    Summary: Discusses the sport of extreme waterskiing, describing some of
the trick steps and aerials as well as safety concerns.
    Includes bibliographical references (p. 31) and index.
    ISBN 0-7368-2155-4 (hardcover)
    1. Water skiing—Juvenile literature. 2. Extreme sports—Juvenile literature.
[1. Water skiing. 2. Extreme sports.] I. Title: Extreme waterskiing moves.
II. Title. III. Series.
GV840. S5F57 2004
796.3'5—dc21   2002156581

Editorial Credits
James Anderson, editor; Jason Knudson, book designer; Jo Miller, photo
    researcher; Karen Risch, product planning editor

Photo Credits
Bruce Coleman Inc./David Madison, 20
Larry Prosor, 16, 28
PhotoDisc, Inc., 4(inset), 10(inset), 18(inset), 26(inset)
Unicorn Stock Photos/Aneal Vohra, 10
USA Water Ski/Scott Atkinson, cover, 4, 7, 8, 13, 14, 15, 18, 21, 23, 25, 26, 29

1 2 3 4 5 6 08 07 06 05 04 03

Table of Contents

Learn about:

How waterskiing was invented

Water-ski styles

Toe-hold straps

Chapter One

Waterskiing

Many pro water-skiers train for more than one event. Chris Parrish, the 2002 Masters Men's Slalom champion, trains for just one. In April 2002, he put 2,700 miles (4,345 kilometers) on his truck driving from his home in Orlando, Florida, to train with his coach, 45 miles (72 kilometers) away. He practiced slalom skiing every day.

Parrish competed with some of the world's best slalom skiers at the 2002 Masters tournament. His many hours of practice paid off. Parrish came away from the event with his first career Masters title.

History

Waterskiing was invented in Minnesota in 1922. Ralph Samuelson first tried to water-ski on two pieces of a barrel. The barrel pieces did not work, so he built his own water-skis.

Samuelson used two boards. He boiled and bent the tips to make them curve upward. He attached straps to hold his feet in place. Samuelson skied on Lake Pepin behind his brother's boat. The fastest they could go was 20 miles (32 kilometers) per hour.

Types of Waterskiing

People water-ski for recreation and in competitions. Water-skiers begin by riding on two skis. This is called riding combo. After they are skilled at riding combo, many water-skiers try riding slalom. Slalom skiers put both feet onto one ski. To ride slalom, skiers start on one ski, or drop one ski during the ride.

Skilled water-skiers compete in tournaments. Slalom, tricks, and jumping are three areas of competition.

Barefoot waterskiing, wakeboarding, and kneeboarding are also types of waterskiing. Kneeboarders kneel on a wide board. Barefoot skiers ride across the water without skis. Wakeboarders use a board similar to a snowboard. Wakeboarding competitions have become popular in recent years.

Ralph Samuelson invented waterskiing in 1922.

Types of Water-skis

Water-skis come in different sizes and shapes. Children use short skis. Children's skis are about 48 inches (122 centimeters) long. Most adult water-skis are 63 to 68 inches (160 to 173 centimeters) long and 8 inches (20 centimeters) wide.

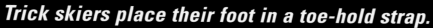
Trick skiers place their foot in a toe-hold strap.

Some water-skiers use combos. This pair of skis has one regular ski and one slalom ski. Each ski has a fin underneath the back of the ski. The fins help a skier steer the skis.

Just like snow skis, water-skis also have bindings. These straps hold a water-skier's feet on the skis. Each regular ski has only one binding. The slalom ski has two bindings. Most bindings are made of foam. Foam bindings form to skier's feet. Some water-skis have rubber bindings. Many skiers think that foam bindings hold a skier's feet in place better than rubber bindings.

Towropes and Handles

Most waterskiing towropes are 75 feet (23 meters) long. Towropes are made of a strong material that does not stretch. The towrope has a handle made of aluminum.

Trick towropes have a separate handle called a toe-hold strap. Trick skiers put their toes in the strap. They do spins and other tricks with one foot in the handle.

Slalom skiers ski around buoys.

Learn about:

- **Slalom speeds**

- **Trickers**

- **Cracking the whip**

Waterskiing Moves

Before water-skiers learn extreme moves, they first master basic moves. Some of these moves are slalom, surface tricks, aerials, and jumps.

Riding Slalom

Slalom water-skiers ride from side to side across the boat's wake. The wake is the V-shaped trail of waves left behind when a boat passes. Waves are created on each side of a wake.

Slalom skiers move out of the wake by leaning back and turning the ski. This is called tracking. If the skier leans to one side and pulls back on the rope, it creates spray.

In competitions, buoys are arranged in a zigzag pattern. Skiers take turns winding through the buoys. The boat speeds up 2 miles (3.2 kilometers) per hour each time the skier takes a turn. The fastest the boat may go is 36 miles (58 kilometers) per hour.

Slalom skiers do not let their skis ride flat on the surface. A flat ride is not easy to control. Skiers move their skis from one edge to another.

Skiers bend their knees and ankles. Relaxed knees and ankles let water-skiers absorb the bumps as they ride over the wake.

During competition, skiers are required to use a shortened towrope. Using a shorter towrope makes swerving through the buoys more difficult.

Trick Waterskiing

Trick water-skiers are called trickers. These skiers ski combo or slalom. Trickers slip a foot into a toe-hold strap to do toe tricks. Trickers also do hand passes. Hand passes are tricks done with the handle held in the athlete's hands.

Trickers do surface tricks and aerials. Surface tricks also are called water turns. The skis are on the water when water turns are performed. Aerial tricks are also called wake turns. The water-skis are in the air during wake turns.

Trickers use the toe-hold strap to do toe tricks.

Jump skiers earn scores for how far they jump.

Jump Waterskiing

In the jumping event, jump skiers cut from side to side behind the boat before they reach the ramp. This is called cracking the whip. Cracking the whip helps the skier go faster.

The faster skiers go, the farther they can jump. Some jump skiers reach speeds of 60 miles (97 kilometers) per hour before they hit the ramp. The best jumpers fly 230 feet (70 meters) or more beyond the edge of the ramp.

Jump water-skiers still hold on to the towrope.

Extreme Waterskiing Slang

chop—rough water

combo—a set of two water-skis, a regular ski and a slalom ski; to ride combo is to ride on both skis.

fanny dunk—sitting down or falling back on any jump landing

header—fall forward

hit it—a water-skier's signal for the boat driver to go

jumpers—a set of long, sturdy skis for jumping

tricks—a set of short skis for doing tricks

180s are water turns.

Learn about:

- Surface tricks
- Aerials
- Combinations

Chapter Three

Extreme Waterskiing Moves

Water-skiers do water turns such as 180s, 360s, and side slides. A 180 is a half turn. After turning, the skier faces backward. A 360 is a 180, plus another half turn to return to ski facing forward. A side slide is riding the skis sideways behind the boat.

Trick water-skiers also perform wake turns. These tricks are done in the air. Step-overs, wake step-overs, and wake flips are wake turns. Other wake turns are ski line tricks, toe-hold side slides, and helicopters.

A skier can do a toe-hold after a step-over 540.

Step-Overs

A step-over line trick is done when a skier lifts a leg over the towrope. Step-overs can be done with a toe-hold or a hand pass.

A skier holds the rope between the legs while riding backward during a step-over 180.

A step-over 360 is a step-over 180 plus a turn back to the forward position. A step-over 540 is a 180 plus a 360-degree turn. The skier is facing backward at the end of this trick.

A wake step-over is a step-over line trick done on the wake. In a wake step-over 180, the skier turns toward the wake. The skier rides the upward curve of the wake and jumps. The skier then spins midair and returns to the water, facing the opposite direction. A wake double step-over 360 is a step-over 180 and a wake step-over combined.

Skiers can perform step-overs on a wake.

Ski Line Tricks

Ski line tricks can also be wake turns if they are done above the water. During these tricks, skiers rotate over the towrope with both feet.

Skiers perform ski line 180s. During this trick, skiers do a one-half spin over the towrope. Skiers face backward after completing a 180.

360s, 540s, and 720s are also ski line tricks. During 360s, skiers spin over the towrope once. When doing a 540, skiers make one and one-half rotations over the towrope. Skiers make two full 360 spins during a 720.

During a wake flip back full twist, skiers do a backward flip off the wake, followed by a full twist. A twist is a sideways spin.

Other ski line tricks are the toe-hold side slide and the helicopter. During a toe-hold side slide, skiers perform a side slide with a foot in the toe-hold strap. While doing a helicopter, a skier makes a 360 vertical spin over the towrope. The skis must not touch the water for a helicopter move to count during a competition.

Ski line tricks involve spins.

Combinations

Trick skiers often combine wake flips, step-overs, and wraps together. A wrap is when the skier spins and allows the rope to wrap briefly around them. The skier then lets go of the rope to do a rotation. Skiers are able to rotate several times in the air after they let go of the rope.

Combination moves were invented when water-skiers became skilled at water turns and wake turns. Skiers began to do small moves together between the wakes. Skiers soon were good at water turn combinations. They wanted to do more challenging moves. Skiers then combined water turn combinations with wake turns. Soon, skiers were doing water turn and wake turn moves combined.

Small tricks put together are combination tricks.

25

Helmets are required for jump skiing.

Learn about:

- **Personal flotation devices**
- **Wetsuits**
- **How to fall**

26

Chapter Four

Safety

The proper equipment is required during waterskiing competitions. Most water-skiers also wear protective gear while practicing.

Protective Gear

All water-skiers must wear Coast Guard approved personal flotation devices, or PFDs. These devices keep a water-skier afloat in deep water. They also protect the skier's upper body during a fall.

Many skiers wear wetsuits. These suits are worn because of their thick foam padding. Not all wetsuits keep water-skiers dry. Most wetsuits are worn as PFDs.

Pro water-skiers also wear other safety equipment. They wear gloves to protect their hands from blisters. They must wear helmets during jump skiing events.

Water-skiers should tuck and roll when they fall.

Safe Waterskiing

Water-ski instructors teach beginners how to fall. If skiers fall, they should tuck their heads under and roll in the direction of the fall. This position protects skiers' necks and upper bodies from hitting the water.

Water-skiers should avoid shallow water. They could crash on hard rocks. Water-skiers should also avoid skiing too close to the dock or the shoreline. If water-skiers ride close to these areas, they could be injured.

Skiers must practice to do slalom, tricks, and jump skiing safely. Skiers must prove that they can safely do stunts before they can enter most tournaments.

Extreme water-skiers continue to invent new moves. The moves they invent are changing the sport of waterskiing.

Today, more people enjoy waterskiing than ever before. More people are learning the moves that make extreme waterskiing fun.

Proper equipment is necessary for safety.

Words to Know

aluminum (uh-LOO-mi-nuhm)—a light, silver colored metal

buoy (BOO-ee)—a floating marker in a body of water

fin (FIN)—a small metal piece on the bottom of a ski to help with steering

surface (SUR-fiss)—the top of something; surface tricks are performed on top of the water.

towrope (TOE-rohp)—the rope a water-skier hangs onto while skiing; the towrope is attached to a motorboat.

tracking (TRAK-ing)—when a skier moves out of a wake; a skier leans back and turns a ski to track out of a wake.

wake (WAYK)—the V-shaped trail of waves left behind when a boat passes

To Learn More

Oleksy, Walter G. *Barefoot Waterskiing.* Extreme Sports. Mankato, Minn.: Capstone Books, 2000.

Thompson, Luke. *Essential Waterskiing for Teens.* Outdoor Life. New York: Children's Press, 2000.

Tomlinson, Joe. *Extreme Sports: The Illustrated Guide to Maximum Adrenaline Thrills.* New York: Carlton Books, 2002.

Useful Addresses

International Water Ski Federation Headquarters
Postbox 564
6314 Unteraegeri
Switzerland

USA Water Ski
1251 Holy Cow Road
Polk City, FL 33688

Water Ski Canada
304 - 2197 Riverside Drive
Ottawa, ON K1H 7X3
Canada

Internet Sites

Do you want to find out more about extreme waterskiing?
Let FactHound, our fact-finding hound dog, do the research
for you.

Here's how:

1) Visit *http://www.facthound.com*
2) Type in the **Book ID** number: **0736821554**
3) Click on **FETCH IT**.

**FactHound will fetch Internet sites picked by our editors
just for you!**

Index